# HOPE IS A SEED THOUGHT

## Jesus is the Seed of Hope

*Sandra E. Banks*

# HOPE IS A SEED THOUGHT

## Jesus is the Seed of Hope

Unlock Hidden Treasures from God's Word

*A*dvantage
BOOKS

# Sandra E. Banks

*Hope is a Seed Thought – Jesus is the Seed of Hope* by Sandra E. Banks
Copyright © 2024 by Sandra E. Banks
All Rights Reserved.
ISBN: 978-1-59755-832-7

Published by:   ADVANTAGE BOOKS™
                Longwood, Florida, USA
                www.advbookstore.com

Unless indicated in context of the chapters, Scripture taken from the NEW KING JAMES VERSION®. Copyright© 1982 by Thomas Nelson, Inc. Used by permission. All rights reserved.

**Library of Congress Catalog Number: 2025931820**

| | |
|---|---|
| **Name:** | Banks, Sandra E., Author |
| **Title:** | *Hope is a Seed Thought – Jesus is the Seed of Hope*<br>by Sandra E. Banks<br>Advantage Books, 2024 |
| **Identifiers:** | ISBN:  Paperback: 9781597558327 |
| **Subjects:** | RELIGION: Christian Life – Inspirational |

First Printing: April 2025
25 26 27 28 29 30 31 32    10 9 8 7 6 5 4 3 2 1

# Table of Contents

## CONCLUSION

*Sandra E. Banks*

# Thank You

I would like to take this opportunity to say thank you so very much for making this journal of inspiration your choice today. I pray that you will find it uplifting as you maintain the faith, building your hope on the things that are spiritual and eternal rather than just the earthly dreams you aspire. Never give up hope in Jesus Christ because He is our savior and He will never give up on you. God's hope is a guarantee that without a shadow of doubt your blessing is on the way. No one is exempt from the trials of this world neither the testing of their faith. I can honestly say that I was tested as I struggled with the patience to write these inspirational messages. It took me over 2 ½ years to finally bring these messages to a close. Even then I found myself writing and rewriting continuously adding more and more to this book. If that wasn't enough of a struggle, I had to force myself to write and maneuver with the distraction of a pandemic where sickness and death was all around me. Knowing that the coronavirus, yes COVID-19, was a deadly infectious disease that has swept across the global world without a known cure or vaccine was a huge distraction. I felt myself using that as an excuse to slow my pace instead of wrapping the writings up. I had to remind myself of one thing and that is even in the face of sickness and death, the love of God toward us has provided believers with the strength we need to keep our focus on the prize that awaits us. As a born-again believer, I know that God has the victory over everything. I have no human control or authority over any of it. All I had to do was put God first, seek his face and pray, that way there was never any need to worry. God has not given believers the spirit of fear, therefore keep the faith and pray. God's love provides victory to overcome any thing in this world.

Always have faith in God and hope in His son, Jesus Christ and be encouraged by the writings of the Apostle Paul when he wrote, *"I can do all things through Christ who strengthens me" (Phil. 4:13 NKJV)*. "There hath no temptation taken you but such as is common to man: but God is faithful, who will not suffer you to be tempted above that ye are able; but will with the temptation also make a way to escape, that ye may be able to bear it" (*I Corinthians 10:13 KJV*).

Thank you so much!

# Introduction To the Journal

This journal is a creation of love for those who are hurting spiritually, physically, mentally and financially. My desire is that each message and scripture will motivate and inspire you as well as renew your hope in Jesus Christ's ability to hear and answer your prayer even in the middle of any difficult situation in your life. When you allow yourself to commit to a daily routine of worship with God, you will begin to experience a change in your personal growth and development in the Word of God. You will also become empowered and gain self-awareness in your ability to witness to others about the goodness of Jesus. As you read through each page, I pray you will have the necessary tools to move forward as you press through all the hurt and the pain with the aid of the Holy Spirit.

Daily reading of the messages and scriptures will serve as your personal connection to Jesus Christ in addition to committing at least one scripture to memory, even if you have to reflect on the same passage over and over again. I pray that you can surrender full control of your life, your heart, mind and soul to the Lord.

By the time you complete the daily journal readings and reach that final page you will have a better insight and an understanding of the Hope-Seed and how it all works together for the good of God's people. You will understand God's desire for obedience and trust in His Word. Last but not least, why you can ask God for what you want and the promises God has available just for you. The idea is to increase your faith and to move toward the pathway of a renewed joy. You will want to make time to give God the glory, honor and praise He deserves. Most of all, I hope that you will began to read and understand God's Holy Word better. If you have already established a relationship with God, you can also use these messages as a practical teaching tool to aid you in your discussions with others about your hope in Jesus Christ and His presence living inside of you. By all means, I challenge you to meditate on the questions at the end of each message and take the opportunity to reflect on the scriptures and find others that will support the thoughts based on the Bible.

# Dedication

This book is dedicated to my children, whom I have the greatest hope and love for as well as a deep appreciation and admiration. Several years ago, before my late husband passed, he would say that we could write a book about our life experiences. For some unknown reason those stories never seemed to get off the ground. In the meantime, it was my children that made me put things into the right perspective. They gave me a very special place in their lives both individually and collectively. Never in a million years did I know just how much they appreciated me and that I would be inspired to write a book of inspirational messages regarding the hope that God provides to us. God has supplied me with so much help to endure my trials and tribulations and that is why I dedicate this journal of inspirational messages to my children. As I look back on my life with my son and daughters, I'm thankful for the special bond we share. We have the love of God living inside of us, allowing us to share our goals and communicate God's love to others. I hope that remaining Christ-like will always be their number one priority in life. Love begins on the inside and in my opinion should start in the privacy of our homes; then love should spread/be disbursed abroad. God is love and his love should always shine and exuberate outside of us from within.

As a result of God's gift of children, I have the ability to write about this wonderful hope I have found in Christ Jesus. I thank God for giving me loving, kind, humble and generous children who have a loving, kind and compassionate disposition toward others. Our bond is built on faith, hope and the love of God. Right now, I have the faith to share these pages of inspiration knowing that God will produce an abundance of blessings by the promises He has made to His children.

If you have faith the size of a mustard seed and believe in your heart that Christ died for you, then you are able to ask for anything and God will hear and answer your prayer. Therefore, I dedicate this book to my loving children for the love and affection they continue to extend to me. God loves you and so do I. You will always have a special place in my heart!

From,

Mom!

# Messages Regarding Hope

*Sandra E. Banks*

# Hope is a Seed Thought

Many times, in our lives we use the word hope to express a desire to have the things we want but, in all honesty, we don't believe we can have them. As I pondered that idea, I began to look for someone else's definition of the word "hope." In my search I found two individuals who took the opportunity to express the word hope in poetry. The first definition is taken from one of the lines of poetry by *Emily Dickinson, an American poet. She wrote*: *"Hope is the thing, with feathers that perches in the soul and sing the tune, without the words and never stop at all"*. Dickinson, in my estimation, explains hope as a thing and has feathers and it can sing. To be honest, I have no idea if that's what she truly believes. However, just as food for thought, there have been times when an idea or song is on my mind and I find myself repeating it over and over without a sound coming out of my mouth. Even when that occurs, I'm not sure I can equate that idea with God's hope.

The second poet, A*lfred Tennyson, a British poet* wrote these words: *"Hope smiles from the threshold of the year to come whispering it will be better." In my opinion,* Tennyson had a two-fold revelation concerning his description of hope. He wrote, hope smiles into the future. When we are looking forward to a productive new year and or better future then I can imagine a smile on our faces. He said hope also approaches the future with a whisper as well. *Now I have to say that they both sound pretty good and even convincing to the itching ear. I think the reason being is because as humans we look forward to the future or to a new season or an even better new year every year.* By whatever means, in each of their thoughts, they have come up with their definition or interpretation and a different way to present the word hope to us.

Jesus however presents hope, His hope, in a very different manner. It is clear that there is no doubt or room for interpretation. Hope is based on a relationship with our Lord which in my opinion is considered a seed-thought. Hope lies deep within the heart and soul of every true believer. It is presented as our blessed hope and it can definitely be seen from afar, from a distance by way of the inner workings of the heart. The inner workings are to bring forward a clean heart of God who sent His only son; Jesus Christ our Messiah. Jesus is our hope for the future. I have two (2) questions for you; 1. What is your definition of hope? 2. Can this kind of hope be seen by anyone?

*Matthew recorded Jesus as saying, "For everyone that asks receives, and he who seeks finds and to him who knocks it will be opened" (Matthew 7:8 NKJV).*

*"For we are saved by hope: but hope that is seen is not hope: for what a man seeth, why doth he yet hope for."(Romans 8:24).*

Discuss your definition of hope and compare it to Matthew 7:8 above or any other scripture that comes to mind.

# Hope Manifest itself by Faith

Take a glance at another interpretation of Hope as an anticipated thought which has been planted in the very heart of the believer. Hope says you will have whatever it is you desire if you really believe it. Hope clearly allows you to see the invisible and expect the impossible. Although it cannot be seen with the naked eye, you can see it like an illuminated pathway guiding you through the shadows of darkness. Hope also places you in a futuristic timeline as it slowly materializes before your eyes. This, my friend, is why it is called the hope seed-thought. It only works when you begin to exercise your faith to the fullest and afterwards it becomes a manifestation of a reality that is already in progress. In other words, hope takes on a physical presence after you develop a sincere, intense conversation with God through prayer.

*For we are saved by hope: but hope that is seen is not hope: for what a man seeth, why doth he yet hope for? But if we hope for that we see not, then do we with patience wait for it" (Romans 8:24-25).*

Discussion: How has Hope manifested itself in your life?

*Sandra E. Banks*

# Will Hope Grow?

The answer to that question is yes. Hope will grow because it is a seed and the seed does grow. The seed will grow to produce the same as any fruit bearing plant whether in a private garden or on a farm. Like a farmer, we must accept the responsibility for the way our seed produces just as the fruit that is provided for the masses. In the case of a Christian, this seed we are discussing is a thought. It is not tangible and it is only seen from the outpouring through our hearts (the central part of our imagination). The seed is definitely capable of growth in the lives of all Christians. In addition, God is the provider of this seed and has placed it in our custody. We have been designated as its personal caregiver or caretaker. Just like a farmer takes personal pride, care and responsibility for his crops we must do the same for our inner seed.

Let me add this to your memory bank, the seed I refer to is your thought process and this seed does not need to be planted by you. You are a representative of the earth of which God created the first man, Adam. Human creation began when God formed man of the dust of the ground, and breathed into his nostrils the breath of life; and man became a living soul (Genesis 2:7). The seed we are discussing was planted by Jesus inside of you, the earth. Just as everyone has been given a measure of faith, in respect to believers, you have been given this seed of hope.

The Christian possesses an overwhelming amount of power which comes from God who is our Father. The development of the seed greatly depends on the work a person will contribute for the growth of his/her seed. Christians have been given power to be the best caretaker he/she can be. For that very reason, it is necessary to show God how loyal you are beginning with your belief, your faith, your love, your trust and your obedience to Him. You can observe the maturity of the seed as you increase in the knowledge of our Lord and Savior, Jesus Christ. If you want growth and a healthy relationship with God you must nurtured the seed as it is developed through constant and continuous communication. Did you remember to offer the seed back to the giver and provider, who is the seed's personal nutritionist? This offering is your acknowledgement that God is the true owner of the seed and it is by His grace we receive His blessings. God provided the instructions on how to care for the seed with an early morning wake up call. Therefore, you must read His Word and have absolutely no time to be idle.

The caretaker (that's you) is responsible to get your work done before the sun shines bright and before it goes down. In doing this, you are assured that the seed of hope will produce an abundance as God begins to shower you with His blessings (increasing the faith, helping others, spreading the gospel and receiving your great harvest). God has given everyone a measure of faith and He knows who will exercise that faith to the fullest. Never allow yourself to become negligent of your responsibilities. If you become negligent the hope-seed is in jeopardy of losing its positive influence and its state of security. Sometimes we lose our focus becoming preoccupied with other interest of the world. Always remember these words, *"But seek ye first the kingdom of God, and His righteousness; and all these things shall be added unto you" (Matthew 6:33).* You can rest assure as you wait with patience, keep the faith and pray, you will reap the fruit of your labor. Never forget to thank God daily and praise Him for all His goodness. Always trust and obey, for in doing so, the outcome will be a pouring out of God's great generosity toward you. To your surprise you will never know when or where the seed will produce, but it will!

*"In the morning sow your seed, and in the evening do not withhold your hand; For you do not know which will prosper, either this or that or whether both alike will be good" (Ecclesiastes 11:6 NKJV).*

Discussion: In Ecclesiastes 11:6 above, is the seed in this verse relative to monetary gain? If it is, how does that seed grow in comparison to your seed-thought?

*Sandra E. Banks*

# God's Seed Produces through Prayer

Waiting and watching for the production of the seed is not an easy thing to do. The growth of the seed seems so far away for two reasons, 1. the seed needs constant prayer while it is in its early stages of development. When a seed is planted into the ground it is dead but life comes to it during the nurturing period. When Jesus died for believers he rose because of the power of God, His heavenly father. 2. You can't force the production of your seed. You must keep the faith even when it seems impossible and even when you feel desperate and feel the need to call on another to help you. You've got to mature and that takes a lot of time.

Feeling uptight and thinking that your seed will not mature as fast as you want it to is a natural thing for any human because we are impatient as well as imperfect human beings. However, when the time is right and the harvest is ready the seed will produce and rest assured, it will be great. Not because you are a farmer but you resemble the occupation of the farmer. You need time to grow so don't rush it, take your time.

*"Pray in the Spirit at all times and on every occasion" (Ephesians 6:18 NKJV).*

*"And let us not grow weary while doing good: for in due season, we shall reap, if we do not lose heart" (Galatians 6:9 NKJV).*

Discussion: Give examples when prayer was productive for you and or beneficial for someone you know.

*Sandra E. Banks*

# Proceed with Caution

The seed requires you to use precautionary measures to make sure it gets its proper nourishment in an effort to produce more than you could ever imagine. The key for this kind of nourishment is constant, persistent communication with our heavenly Father (that's called prayer). *"One day Jesus told his disciples a story to show that they should always pray and never give up"* (Luke 18:1 *NLT)*.

God is the rightful owner of the seed as I explained to you earlier. The seed has only been entrusted to your care to look after, similar to the Parable of the talents (Matthew 25:14-30). The seed I make reference to, in its present state will never be visible to the naked eye because it is invisible. Intangibles will never be seen, you will never eat them, you will never physically touch them in your harvest but by faith you will repeat the benefit from them. It is just as the working of the Holy Spirit that comes into the believer's life to perform a change in him/her, we do not see that force working in us but, it is there. Therefore by the power of God, the seed-thought works in a similar fashion. That in itself is a mystery and in the natural mind is hard to comprehend. Therefore, it is incumbent upon you to communicate the seed back to the giver (the owner, God) while clinging to your faith with patience.

God in his infinite wisdom and knowledge knows what you need before you ask but, His desire is that you ask him for it anyway. Trust in God, it is imperative that you take caution and do this for the security of the seed that is within. God is always interested in just how your faith in Him has developed as well.

*"And we desire that every one of you do show the same diligence to the full assurance of hope unto the end: That ye be not slothful but*

*followers of them; who through faith and patience inherit the promise"* (Hebrews 6:11-12). Blessed is the man that trusteth in the Lord, and whose hope the Lord is (Jeremiah 17:7).

Discussion: How are blessings received by believers? Support with scripture.

# A Far Away Scene

Now let us turn to a particular situation or circumstance that will serve as a guide in helping to further define hope. Some time ago I came across a lady who believed that she was a very strong-willed person, in her opinion. After trying to do things her way by setting goals she had for her future career and marriage, she was certain that she was looking into her very own future. This was not strong will but a strong belief in the power of the almighty God.

She made a list of her expectations for the person she wanted to marry. She knew the qualities that this man must have (love and a respect for her), a tender and caring person, dedicated, loyal and devoted to her no matter what the circumstance. He would be open minded and honest, able to communicate and love God. Of course knowing that no one is perfect. She had faith and a strong belief in God honoring her request. She also desired to be that person to her mate as well. Even if it took years, she would wait for it because her faith would never let her give up hope. It is clear that faith, trust and belief are the main components needed to satisfy the hope in anticipating unforeseen earthly desires as well.

God can completely satisfy our desires and make them a reality. It is not just a dream but, it is the hope of the future as seen from a distance that has not yet taken place. This is clearly stated in the book of Matthew, "But seek ye first the kingdom of God and His righteousness and all these things shall be added unto you" (Matthew 6:33).

In the same manner, hope can be described as an anticipated thought planted into the heart of the believer. It's saying that you will have whatever it is you desire if you believe in God and the work He has done in Jesus Christ. You must believe that Jesus is the son of God who died for the sins of the world. He was sent by His father to take away all sin. Jesus is also the hope of salvation. You've never physically seen Jesus, haven't witnessed any of the marvelous miracles, but you call on him when you need him. You also have hope that he is coming back to receive you into his Kingdom for a better life. My friend that is hope from within.

Hope allows you to see what you want from afar (from a distance) and it never stops. This, my friend, is called the hope seed-thought. When you begin to exercise faith, your hope becomes a manifestation of a reality already in progress.

*"Keep on asking, and you will receive what you ask for. Keep on seeking, and you will find. Keep on knocking, and the door will be opened to you" (Matthew 7:7 NLT). "We were given this hope when we were saved (if we already have something, we don't need to hope for it. But if we look forward to something we don't yet have, we must wait patiently and confidently" (Romans 8:24-25 NLT).*

Listen, brothers and sisters, ladies and gentlemen; we also wait with patience anticipating the arrival of Jesus when He return to earth for his bride (the church). That my friend is our greatest hope in anticipation without ever having seen Jesus. We have never heard him declare to our faces that he will return. We have only God's Word, yet we believe with faith which produces our greatest hope for a brighter future.

Discuss: "Hope seen from afar"

# Cultivate the Seed

Hope is a seed that has been given to you to cultivate (to develop). Reading God's word with praises and praying early with thanksgiving is one way to cultivate the seed as well as to secure the production of it in hope. This seed-thought may seem repetitive but it is an important fact and it can't be stressed enough. In ancient times, people dealt with agriculture and animals as a way of life and survival, they were so to speak farmers in their own right. Not only was agriculture the way in those days but in the beginning, Adam was made from the dust so planting, cultivating, sowing and reaping almost seem natural to man.

True story, for a short period of time my home was in Salinas, CA. My commute to work and church were located in the Monterey Bay area and that was nothing short of a 30-mile drive, one way. During the ride I would pass miles and miles of farm land to the right and to the left of me. I could see the farmers working hard for the production not for just a mere harvest but for a grand harvest.

Just like those farmers, everyone who is a believer in Christ must do their part in sowing and reaping their harvest. We must approach God while it is early and everything is very still and quiet. We must make time not only in the early morning but, at noon day and night. However, there is always something we must not do and that is never become complacent after that seed has been planted waiting for the production of that seed. In other words, keep yourself occupied/stay busy doing something constructive. Don't allow your mind to become idle while waiting for the outcome of your labor (that is in your prayer and praise) to produce the fruit. Your investment is what has been planted in you which makes reaping the seed's harvest worth the wait because your harvest is promised to be a great one.

*"In the morning sow your seed, and in the evening do not withhold your hand; For you do not know which will prosper, either this or that or whether both alike will be good" (Ecclesiastes 11:6 NKJV).*

Discuss: What assurances do we have in regard to the belief that prayer will produce a blessing? What is prayer? How can you cultivate something you can't see? Support your answers with scripture.

# Be Content in Your Hope

*Sandra E. Banks*

# A Feeling of Hopelessness

There will be times in life when you feel what you are doing is hopelessly waiting in expectation for the Lord to hear and answer your prayer request. When will God answer your prayer, after all didn't the Lord say to let your request be made known unto Him? You say, if only God would honor your request and give you what you've been asking. Maybe you found yourself just standing, gazing into the sky like I did saying, if God could really hear me, He would answer my cry. I thought it would be so wonderful if it would just happen to me at the very time I wanted it to happen. At that point in my life, I was desperate and I didn't know what to do. I knew for certain that what I wanted, God had not met that need. But I can honestly say don't give up and don't become discouraged, you are not alone. God in his own time will provide the answer to all of your problems because He has compassion for you and is merciful and just. God will always love you and He does hear and will answer your prayer.

*"You can pray for anything, and if you have faith, you will receive it" (Matthew 21:22 NLT).*

*"Don't worry about anything; instead, pray about everything. Tell God what you need, and thank him for all he has done" (Philippians 4:6 NLT).*

Discussion: Why should we go to God when we are feeling hopelessly alone? What does God say about worry? Discuss why we shouldn't worry!

*Sandra E. Banks*

# Stay Positive

Keep the faith and add some peace with your hope as you begin to wait patiently and pray. Make it your mission to strive to be positive while you meditate and pray during your labor because it is one of the keys to producing success. Don't allow yourself to get upset and become frustrated thinking about situations that are not in your control. It is an unnecessary waste of your precious time. Don't allow your mind to stray to those things you did that were unsuccessful in the past. This will only arouse many unfavorable thoughts. Negative thoughts bring about negative feelings and emotions which can oftentimes lead to both hurt and anger. Negativity, in some circumstances, can produce a hindrance in what God has planned for your life. Focus on your prayer life and be encouraged. Everything is in God's hands and he is in control of everything. Just as we wait for the Lord's return with patience, we have to do the same in our hope. God is mighty in power; all you have to do is wait on the Lord and he will show up just when the time is right.

*"You too, must be patient. Take courage for the coming of the Lord is near" (James 5:8 NLT). "Wait patiently for the Lord. Be brave and courageous. Yes, wait patiently for the Lord" (Psalm 27:14 NLT).*

Discuss: Ways to remain positive while waiting.

*Sandra E. Banks*

# Be Practical While You Wait

So, you think it's your time to be prosperous and you want to have it right now. Everyone around you appears to be doing well and you're only making ends meet. It's a real struggle for you and you know it could be a whole lot better. You are desperate and impatiently waiting for that one person everyone has heard of and talked about (Jesus the Christ) to step into your life and rescue you.

*Who told you waiting is easy? Quite the contrary, it is* not easy to wait especially on a Spirit-being (Jesus) to answer you! The great discovery for me concerning waiting is that it is practical. It requires you to be content in the situation you are facing. You will only become patient with practice and a good way to practice is in your daily prayer. Along with prayer, we must learn to do what the Apostle Paul said the secret to waiting is in the book of Philippians. Read it below, you must meditate continuously on good things.

*"And now dear brothers and sisters one final thing; Fix your thoughts on what is true, and honorable, and right, and pure, and lovely, and admirable. Think about things that are excellent and worthy of praise. Keep putting into practice all you have learned and received from me—everything you heard from me and saw me doing. Then the God of peace will be with you." (Philippians* 4:8-9 NLT).

Discuss: Help with Practical waiting

# You Will Understand It Better

Christians who feel they are well seasoned in Christianity often offer what they feel are encouraging words or advice to those who are weary. Such words as; "He may not come when you want him but he's always on time." If that has been directed to you, then your response to them might be something like this:

1) Who is this person you are talking about?

2) What time will he show-up?

3) Is this Jesus the intercessor, the go between God and man?

4) Is this an old wise fable?

5) Can you show me the scripture; He may not come when you want him?

The fact of the matter is that the truth of God's Word has been declared in no uncertain terms, Jesus is the mediator in the Bible. Jesus is the person who stands in the presence of God on behalf of all believers. The answer to one of those questions is a fact and the truth cannot be disputed. Jesus has always stood before His father on our behalf. He pleads our case according to the scriptures and His father will respond to you with an answer. You don't have to be discouraged and grow weary in the process because Jesus has promised a harvest and, in that season, when the time is right, it will be worth the wait. You may not understand it while you are in your valley but help is on the way. All you have to do is to keep the faith and do the very best in giving God both the honor and the praise he deserves. It is my prayer that you believe with your heart what has been written in the perfect Word of God and when the time is right, you will understand it better each day of your life.

*"And let us not grow weary while doing good; for in due season, we shall reap, if we do not lose heart" (Galatians 6:9 NKJV).*

Discuss: What is meant by waiting for due season and answer questions 1, 2 and 3 above with supporting scripture.

# Prayer Works

*Sandra E. Banks*

# God is Waiting to hear from You

In this life we encounter many losses, through sickness and death, loss of jobs, loss of friendship caused by disappointments, loss of spouses, a trusting and faithful companion, or simply loss of time available to you to spend with a loved one. In all honesty, sometimes in these situations we fail to be specific with God in our prayer life. If you need more time, then ask God for more time. If it's another chance, He is a God of another chance. If we just trust in the Lord and place our confidence in him, the Lord will hear our faintest cry. Always thank Him and confess your love to him with all your heart, your soul and your mind. Give God the highest praise, honor Him and glorify His holy name. Take a little time out of your busy schedule and just call out God's name.

Obedience and communication (prayer) is another key to God's heart and he will help you with any problem you may have. God is compassionate and wants to grant you another blessing and another chance. He knows you are not able to handle the situation all by yourself. God desires to have a conversation with you in sincerity, just ask him and he will provide.

*"Trust in the Lord with all your heart; do not depend on your own understanding. Seek His will in all you do, and he will show you which path to take" (Proverbs 3:5-6 NLT). "Let the whole world bless our God and loudly sing His praises: (Psalm 66:8 NLT). "Those who plant in tears will harvest with shouts of joy. They weep as they go to plant their seed, but they sing as they return with the harvest." (Psalm 126:5-6 NLT).*

Discuss: The benefit of Praise, obedience and communication with God

*Sandra E. Banks*

# What God Has Done for Others!

God does not show favoritism to anyone but he does consider a person's motives, the person's disposition and how much that person can bear. Whatever you may think is fair in your mind, you should remember this one thing; it is never how God sees it. We must be totally submissive to God and become close to him. It is imperative to be humble before God and obey his commands. In his own time, he will honor your request and elevate you to higher heights. Confess your sins and ask for God's help in guiding you to live a righteous life.

*In the Book of Romans, it is recorded, "For God does not show favoritism." (Romans 2:11 NLT).*

*Showing partiality is never good, yet some will do wrong for a mere piece of bread." (Proverbs 28:21 NLT).*

Meditate and discuss: Favoritism/Partiality and be truthful in your discussion if you have ever shown favoritism toward an individual.

*Sandra E. Banks*

# Have Faith and Believe in Prayer

We are all God's creation and we need to fellowship with him because He wants to fellowship with us. All human beings possess a need to be in a friendly healthy relationship with someone and although God is spirit, He also desires to have a relationship with His children. We communicate with God through our prayer life. Prayer is the way we have a conversation with Him. Also, we must read God's Holy Bible to become close to Him thereby understanding His thoughts and how to live a righteous life. He created us (His children) in His own image and He loves us unconditionally. Therefore, God hears us and His greatest desire is to answer our prayers.

Prayer should become a sincere practice, a good habit. God expects us to pray and He wants us to come to him in prayer through his son, Jesus Christ. Our faith and belief are the key to all unanswered prayer. There is power in prayer and one of the greatest weapons we can possess. Through prayer we can feel God's strength. *The Spirit of God, who raised Jesus from the dead, lives in all Christians. Just as God raised Christ Jesus from the dead, he will give life to your mortal bodies by this same Spirit that lives within you (Romans 6:10-11)*. Throughout Jesus' ministry in the New Testament, He can be found praying to His Father. Some examples found in scripture are: Jesus prayed before He raised Lazarus from the dead, Jesus taught His disciples how to pray, Jesus prayed in the Garden of Gethsemane, Jesus prayed while on the cross and Jesus prayed and gave thanks to His Father because He recognized that there is tremendous power in prayer!

*The Lord detests the sacrifice of the wicked, but he delights in the prayers of the upright." (Proverbs 15:8 NLT). Jesus said; "I tell you,*

*you can pray for anything, and if you believe that you've received it, it will be yours." (Mark 11:24 NLT).*

Discuss: Prayer and the power of it, also discuss a consistent prayer life and God's reaction to it.

(**HINT:** You may find the answer in a previous discussion)

# Rejoice in Hope

Keep the faith and rejoice in hope as you wait and pray earnestly. You will be productive because of it. Don't get upset which leads to doubt and frustration but, be patient because everything is under God's control. All you have to do is rejoice and wait on the Lord. Talk to God and remind him what his word says and that the whole world is in his hand. While you are waiting, be hopeful don't allow yourself to become desperate or impatience. God knows what you need before you even ask for it but, He wants you to ask for it anyway. So, ask away!

*"May all who are godly rejoice in the LORD and praise his holy name" (Psalm 97:12 NLT).*

*"Don't worry about anything; instead, pray about everything. Tell God what you need, and thank him for all he has done" (Philippians 4:6 NLT).*

Discussion: What is your position regarding praying about anything?

Do you think God wants to hear everything you have to say?

# Pray Unselfishly

As we go through life, facing both good times and bad, it may sometime seem as though we are passing through the land of dry bones and in a place where our thirst can never be quenched. All over the world people were experiencing COVID-19, the coronavirus. As a result I could not imagine the stressfulness those individuals lying in their hospital beds were feeling. Not only were they afraid, but some may even have lost hope of overcoming that battle. As bad as that was, Christians were expected to overcome and reject that feeling and allow prayer to take priority in our lives. We are constantly told that there is so much power in prayer and that it is the same power that raised Jesus from the dead.

I have noticed on several occasions that when I pray things happen and when I completely stop or spend a little less time with God, things slow down for me and even get somewhat worse. I believe if we follow the command of God and obey Him and pray, He will hear and He will answer. If God answers us for one thing, He will surely answer us for another. He does this merely because His grace and mercy has been extended to all even when we don't deserve it. God is not a selfish God and neither should we be that way. In order to be unselfish just as a reminder, we should look out for the wellbeing of others. It is a command of God that we are to pray for one another. I believe in that crucial period of unknown disease many people came together to pray for the lives of others. We are to always extend that same grace to our fellowman as God has extended it to us. That includes praying for each other in good and bad times because it is required and necessary. We are a work-in-progress and are both ambassadors and helpers in the work for the completion of God's kingdom building.

The Word of God says: *"So encourage each other and build each other up, just as you are already doing." (1 Thessalonians 5:11 NLT).*

*"Pray in the Spirit at all times and on every occasion. Stay alert and be persistent in your prayers for all believers everywhere." (Ephesians 6:18 NLT).*

*"Confess your sins to each other and pray for each other so that you may be healed. The earnest prayer of a righteous person has great power and produces wonderful results." (James 5:16 NLT).*

Discussion: What are the benefits of prayer and the benefit of praying for each other?

# Things Not Seen

*Sandra E. Banks*

# Identify Obstacles that Get in Your Way

(a) Distraction, Frustration, Temptation and Trouble

There can be times in life when obstacles show up out of nowhere and they are a total nuisance. They cause turmoil, place hurdles in your way you can't get over. Now you are faced with troubles you did not foresee. Obstacles are there to confuse and camouflage the path God has planned for you. Frustration takes over and your emotions get the better of you. Obstacles appear in places where they have never been before. I'm referring to obstacles that are distractions and temptations that make it so easy for you to stumble and fall. In other words, that is exactly what obstacles are designed to do. They get in the way to blind you and tempt you in an effort to rob you of the blessings of God. But be happy in your hope, God will not allow any obstacles to overtake you or hinder His plans for you.

"The Temptations in your life are no different from what others experience. And God is faithful. He will not allow the temptation to be more than you can stand. When you are tempted, he will show you a way out so that you can endure." (I Corinthians 10:13 NLT).

Discussion: What are some influences and or obstacles that can or have cause distractions in your life?

(b) They Control the Mind

Obstacles show up in many forms but they function as previously stated they are distractions designed to tempt you into becoming evil. You can't see the good for wanting to do the bad (the evil). Evil interferes with the blessing God has promised or at least evil tries to interfere with them. Obstacles are planted in the mind to take control of you and have complete power over your life. In other words, they are there to get you angry, to irritate and to convince you to give up. They are there to distract you from your faith and get you to act in haste. They may even make you feel good but the feeling is only short-term. Therefore, utilize your faith, gain a little knowledge first, then understand that you are not in control of your life and never will be. God is in control of your life and with your faith and the power of the Holy Spirit, be assured; you will remain under God's control.

*"Fools vent their anger, but the wise man quietly hold it back." (Proverbs 29:11 NLT). "Getting wisdom is the wisest thing you can do! And whatever else you do, develop good judgment." (Proverbs 4:7 NLT).*

Open a discussion on Wisdom and how it helps you with self-control

# The Unexpected can be a Test

Unexpected issues arise when you least expect them. They too are a total nuisance. They appear in your life to block you from receiving the benefits resulting from the best laid plan, not yours. They show up to hinder God's plans for your life. You must remember it is not your best laid plans that come to fruition but God's plans and promises on your life. These unexpected issues are the challenges we sometimes face in our lives. Don't get upset or even angry concerning the matter. Be of good cheer and don't be discourage, God may only be using them as a test of your faith, so press forward and stay focused. God is the captain of the ship and he will guide you safely through and help you to remain under control.

*"God is my helper; the Lord is the one who sustains me" (Psalm 54:4 KJV). "And we know that all things work together for good to those who love God, to those who are the called according to His purpose" (Romans 8:28). "These trials are only to test your faith, to see whether or not it is strong and pure. It is being tested as fire test gold and purifies it---and your faith is far more precious to God than mere gold; so, if your faith remains strong after being tried in the test tube of fiery trials, it will bring you much praise and glory and honor on the day of his return" (I Peter 1:7).*

Discussion: Give examples of the testing of your faith

*Sandra E. Banks*

# Anger and Evil

*Sandra E. Banks*

# Anger is Not of God

Anger in my opinion is an incredible ugly evil agent. It is ungodly, and it is used to bring about failure in our lives if it lingers. The characteristics of anger are cursing, murder, wickedness, strife and sin just to name a few. Failure to live the life that God has already planned for us can cause many unnecessary problems in our lives. We must be patient and remain under the control of the Holy Spirit and look to God for direction in our lives. The secret is to remember that unforeseen things will happen in life. However, we have God's power working inside of us to keep and protect us. In order to accomplish any godly endeavor successfully we must remember the words that *Jonah said, "I knew that God was gracious and compassionate, slow to anger and abounding in love, a God who relents from sending calamity" (Jonah 3:10).*

Anger in itself must be put to shame. But we must be prayerfully patient and think before we react, give the Holy Spirit his time to work in us to conquer our anger in order for us to become successes in the eyes of the LORD.

*"My dear brother, understand this; everyone should be quick to listen slow to speak and slow to anger; for human anger does not accomplish God's righteousness" (James 1:19-20 CSB).*

Discuss: Anger and how you deal with it.

*Sandra E. Banks*

# Other Evils We Encounter

Sometimes we find ourselves faced with descriptive evils and all the negativities of this world we inhabit. There will be things we do not see coming until it happens. These evils I'm referring to are not derived from flesh and blood although they are manifested through humans. They appear from the spirit realm. They are the evils that we must be prepared for such as; the spirit of prejudice, opposition, envy, adversity, hatred, rejection, etc. We will always be faced with evil, be assured we do not know where or when evil or disaster will pay us a visit. However, that does not mean we should be caught off guard. Instead, be prepared by investing in fasting and prayer.

"Ship your grain across the sea; after many days you may receive a return. Invest in *seven ventures, yes in eight; you do not know what disaster may come upon the land" (Ecclesiastes 11:1-2 NIV). "For our struggle is not against flesh and blood but, against the rulers, against the authorities, against the powers of this dark world and against the spiritual forces of evil in the heavenly realms"* (Ephesians 6:12 NIV).

Discussion: Explain what or who we struggle against in this world?

# Trust in God

*Sandra E. Banks*

# Trust and Obey

In the earlier pages of this collection of inspirational messages, there is one point I want to bring to your attention and it is a message on the growth and care involved in developing the seed. Now I would like to include another key factor to both growth and development of the hope seed and that is to trust and obey in God by faith. To be happy in Jesus is to trust and obey because there really is no other way.

*Jesus said, "Have faith in God" (Mark 11:22).* This means that you should be willing to obey God for your security and well-being in your life. It's all about you developing in Christ the redeemer of your life. If you are willing, just remember you have security in God for his word is perfect and his promises are true. All you have to do is to trust and obey Him and Him alone. The rewards are overflowing with an abundance of blessings that you won't have enough room to store them. Make it a habit to read the Word of God, constantly thank God, establish a better communication through prayer as well as to honor God with the praise he deserves.

*"Cast all your anxiety on him because He cares for you" (1Peter 5:7NIV).*

*"And without faith it is impossible to please God, because anyone who comes to him must believe that he exists and that he rewards those who earnestly seek him" (Hebrews 11:6 NIV).*

*"Trust in the LORD and do good; dwell in the land and enjoy safe pasture" (Psalm 37:3 NIV).*

Discuss: Faith, Trust and Obedience

*Sandra E. Banks*

# Don't Worry

Worry does not help and since God invested in your life through Jesus Christ, you certainly do not want to put the seed in danger, harm or even loss. Therefore don't be concerned about issues you have little or no control over in your life; to the point of extreme worry. Do you go to bed with them on your mind and wake up with those same thoughts? Is this healthy, can it be that worry is consuming your life? Your Father loves you and he knows about your issues. He will take care of your concerns if you let him; so, don't worry any more.

*Jesus said, "Therefore I say unto you, take no thought for your life, what ye shall eat, or what you shall drink; nor yet for your body, what ye shall put on. Is not the life more than meat, and the body than raiment" (Matthew 6:25 KJV)?*

*"But seek ye first the kingdom of God, and his righteousness; and all these things shall be added unto you" (Matthew 6:33 KJV).*

Discussion: Your thoughts on worry! Find scriptures to support Jesus' thoughts on Worry

*Sandra E. Banks*

# Exhausted and Fatigued

Tell me what you think about having a conversation with a Christian woman or man who knew that they would not have many days left to spend with their spouse. The time was discovered in a dream. As the story goes, a couple were on their way to church holding hands. Suddenly their hands would drop and one of the spouses would hurry along reaching a great arena and continue into the sunset. Unable to keep up, that spouse soon disappeared. This dream was not a one-time occurrence, but happened several times. After having had this dream repeatedly, the Christian thought it was necessary to confront their mate. The frustration was overwhelming besides that, there was another problem brewing. It appeared the spouse's lack of interest in taking their prescribe medications presented itself with yet another issue to address. This drastic stop of meds left the spouse weak and with almost no strength. Seeing the strength leaving the body and knowing everything humanly possible had been done, a conversation had to take place between the two of them.

When you have done the very best that you can, keep the faith and never give up. Don't allow yourself to be worried or upset just keep the faith. God has compassion for his children and he hears their cry. Stand firm in your faith, don't get frustrated and become weary. Remember to ask for God's help, He loves and cares deeply for you.

*"But if you remain in me and my words remain in you, you may ask for anything you want, and it will be granted" (John 15:7 NLT).*

*"And let us not be weary in well doing: for in due season we shall reap, if we do not faint" (Galatians 6:9 KJV).*

Discuss: Frustration and Weariness

*Sandra E. Banks*

# Be Victorious in all Situations

There may come a time when you feel down and out because you are in need, the cupboard is bare and you have hit rock bottom. The love of God's children appears to have vanished and is there any charities or has that disappeared with love too? You might ask yourself; who visits the sick or feed the hungry, who takes care of the widows and the orphans? Is this not the primary duty given to the body of Christ? Of course it is, but don't let that affect you in your most vulnerable situation. God has an answer for those questions and hard situations.

Paul gives us the answer on what to do in that situation or any circumstances of that nature. He wrote, God wants us to be content because he will supply our need. *"I know what it is to be in need and I know what it is to have plenty. I have learned the secret of being content in any and every situation. Whether well fed or hungry, whether living in plenty or in want. I can do all things through Christ which strengthen me" (Philippians 4:12-13 NIV).*

God made a promise to us and the Word says God cannot lie.

*"God is not a man that he should lie; or a son of man, that he might change his mind. Does he speak and not act or promise and not fulfill" (Numbers 23:19 CSB)*

Discuss: What does content in all situations mean to you?

*Sandra E. Banks*

# Contrary to popular Opinion,

(a) God made a Direct Deposited in You

Sometimes it is hard to accept the truth. It may be even painful for us to make decisions based on the truth or even to follow the truth. We must not allow the truth to be our stumbling block. Although living and walking in the truth may seem to be difficult at times, following the truth will never lead you away from Christ, it will make you free. The truth that sets you free is God's holy Word and his illuminating light placed inside of you is under the protection and the authority of the Holy Spirit as a seal and promise of redemption. When Jesus went to Nazareth (His home town) the Bible records Him standing up to read. He was given the book of the prophet Isaiah to read from. Afterward Jesus gave his discourse, telling the people he was anointed to preach, to heal, to recover sight to the blind and to set captives free. Jesus was telling them of God's plan for their lives through His very existence. However, those same people sitting in that synagogue were unable to accept the truth from Jesus because he was just a man, the son of the carpenter Joseph. Jesus was a carpenter, by trade and he was poor. They became angry and plotted to kill Jesus for telling the truth. "A*nd all they in the synagogue, when they heard these things, were filled with wrath" (Luke 4:28 KJV). "And you shall know the truth and the truth shall make you free" (John 8:32 KJV). Then Spake Jesus again unto them, saying, "I am the light of the world: he that followeth me shall not walk in darkness, but shall have the light of life" (John 8:12 KJV). "For ye were sometimes darkness, but now are ye light in the Lord: walk as children of light: For the fruit of the spirit is in all goodness and righteousness and truth" (Ephesians 5:8-9 KJV).*

Discuss: The phrase the Truth and Life

(b) The LORD is your Redeemer

Now is the time to begin practicing a song of praise where you can cry out to the Lord not just in the difficult times but when you are also doing well. Give God the praises he deserves because He really is listening to you when you call. God left us with the third person of the trinity, the Holy Spirit. God carefully sealed us with His Holy Spirit and assigned him with other responsibilities. He is the Spirit of truth in our lives. If you ever feel abandoned, deserted, confused or weak, the Spirit is there to make intercession for you with wordless groans. Just hold on because help is on the way. Isaiah said to the Israelites that the LORD of host is their Redeemer, the Holy One of Israel.

*"Fear not, you will no longer live in shame. Don't be afraid there is no more disgrace for you" "For your Creator will be your husband; the LORD of Heaven's Armies is His name! He is your Redeemer, the Holy One of Israel: the God of all the earth" shall He be called" (Isaiah 54:4-5 NLT).*

Discuss: The Holy One of Israel: The Redeemer.

Do you believe Jesus is our redeemer if so, how would you justify your answer?

What scripture would you use if you needed one?

# What's Your Excuse?

God has made a conscious awareness to all mankind that he exists. Everyone is given an opportunity to be saved because of it. God made possible the removal of all human excuses therefore we have no excuse to be lost in sin. Creation is clearly revealed through God's awesome power and his invisibility is seen in the things that he made from the beginning. His invisible character in this world is revealed in the things that can be seen. If that is true than man is able to see the handiwork of God every day and be a witness that only God could do this. Man has never been able to take credit for anything that the LORD God called into existence. What could be any excuse not to accept God as Lord of heaven and earth?

*"For ever since the world was created, people have seen the earth and sky. Through everything God made they can clearly see his invisible qualities—his eternal power and divine nature. So, they have no excuse for not knowing God" (Romans 1:20 NLT).*

Discussion: What is your proof that God does exist?

*Sandra E. Banks*

# Jesus Doesn't Exclude Anyone

Jesus is your Savior of the world and He is the answer to everything. Jesus does not exclude anyone but, he includes everyone. All you have to do is accept the fact that He is the only one who could do this wonderful act of love. Consequently, you can go to the Father in Jesus'name and ask for anything. The first thing commanded is for you to believe on him and finally to accept His Word. Jesus wants you to personally ask Him for any and everything you need because he is your provider and the personal healer of all diseases.

*But the officer said, "Lord, I am not worthy to have you come into my home. Just say the word from where you are, and my servant will be healed" (Matthew 8:8 NLT). "Keep on asking and you will receive what you ask for. Keep on seeking, and you will find. Keep on knocking, and the door will be opened to you" (Matthew 7:7 NLT).*

Discuss: The kind of love Jesus has for everyone

*Sandra E. Banks*

# Seasons

*Sandra E. Banks*

# Seasons Come and Seasons Go

(a) Seasons Change

Christian's lives are filled with seasons; some are filled with ups while others are filled with downs. There are seasons of prosperity, which produces plenty and, in this season, you are doing well. To whatever extent, you might possibly be in a season of lack, a time when you are in a slump, not doing very well at all. In this season your plenty has vanished and the well has dried up. You may feel a little desperate in this season. You may even begin to feel God doesn't care about you anymore. In that instance you may be tempted to take matters into your hands because God is not moving you fast enough to get you out of this situation.

I'm sure you may have heard somewhere that God designed time with man in mind and that part is correct. However, the real truth of the matter is, how relevant is time to our Creator?

Have you been praying consistently, patiently waiting and reading God's Word? Doing all of the right things right this time. Yet you don't feel things are any better than they were before you entered this new seasonal journey. In fact in some cases you think things appear to be a little worst. By now you want to take matters in your hands but be advised this will only prolong the season and mess up God's plan for you. Be not dismayed, you must remember that seasons do end and the changing of a season brings about many other opportunities and a fresh start to begin again. Just be patient and hold on a little longer. The Bible says, "Even Jesus after being tempted by the devil, when the devil ended all temptation, he departed from him for a season" (Luke 4:13 KJV).

Discussion: Find as much as you can on Seasons and meditate on what you have found and apply it to life in general.

### (b) Seasons involve Separation

Sometimes our season involves a drastic change that warrants a separation or a loss of someone or something. Seasonings may sometime come with tragedy that you won't see. It can also be a time that is very much needed. My hope is that in your season, it will be a new beginning. Hopefully the season will be a welcoming change as well as a positive one. In order to walk into this new start, you may have to leave something or even someone behind. It could be a job, maybe making a move from one house to another or a move across state lines. You may lose a love one, be separated from a family member or someone who has shown themselves as friendly to you. Don't forget about the one who loves to give unsolicited non-constructive advice! All of these can dictate you entering into a new season. If and when any of these occur, always remember the Lord has already prepared you for your season no matter how hard it may seem.

*The psalmist writes: "Oh, the joys of those who do not follow the advice of the wicked or stand around with sinners, or join in with the mockers" (Psalm 1:1 NLT).*

Discuss: Scriptures on seasons and what happens in them good or bad.

# There can be Freedom in another Season

Freedom from the old season is the conclusion of a period of time that is behind you. In another season it is the end of an era and at that time the curtain is at last closing. Doors are opening and opportunities are in the making. God has heard your cry and is making a way for you to make the move. When this takes place, you must move with haste. Your obedience and faith in Jesus is critical to make wise decisions. You may be influenced by others in making a wise decision. Always consult with God before you move. He will let you know that you are free from all obstacles that were allowing the enemy to cloud your mind or to sin and become a prisoner to your evil thoughts. Don't let anyone influence your decision to move. Cleanse your mind from all evil by adding good wholesome thoughts to it. Consult God first above all and move into your season.

*"When Jesus had lifted up himself, and saw none but the woman, he said unto her, Woman, where are those, thine accusers? Hath no man condemned thee?*

*She said, No man, Lord. And Jesus said unto her, neither do I condemn thee: go, and sin no more" (John 8:10-11 KJV).*

*The Apostle Paul said, "Finally, brethren, whatsoever things are true, whatsoever things are honest, whatsoever things are just, whatsoever things are pure, whatsoever things are lovely, whatsoever things are of good report; if there be any virtue, and if there be any praise, think on these things" (Philippians 4:8 KJV).*

Discussion: Have you experienced a season of change?

# Identifying the Season

There are many subtle ways God will implement a change in the season for your life. You will find yourself facing a number of situations. For example; you may be surrounded by negative people. In most cases negativity can usher in unhealthy influences in your life. It could also be someone who you have confided in and you have allowed them to give you their personal opinions which may have affected your thinking. Maybe there are other obstacles that have played a part in hindering your growth and delayed your progress in life. If you can relate to anyone of these examples, you have now recognized something I call blessing blockers. These are a few good reasons for a seasonal change to take place. It is a good time to move.

Maybe you are in your own way and haven't turned it over to Jesus. What better way to get rid of that old baggage then through a change in your season of turmoil. You can rest assure there will always be something or someone you must leave behind in order to enter into your new season. If you stay there long enough, God will in His own time and His own way move you. It will be hard and you may even resist, but when you do move you will find it most advantageous. What about it? Is it time to close that curtain and open the door to a healthy relationship/life with Jesus. It is written in the Bible, "For the wisdom of the world is foolishness with God. God speaks to us through His Holy Word all you have to do is listen and apply it to your life.

*The Lord had said unto Abram, "leave your native country, your relatives, your father's family and go to the land that I will show you. I will make you into a great nation. I will bless you and make you famous, and you will be a blessing to others" (Genesis 12:1-2 NLT).*

*"We destroy every proud obstacle that keeps people from knowing God. We capture their rebellious thoughts and teach them to obey Christ" (II Corinthians 10:5 NLT).*

Discussion: Have you recognized the time to move? What did you do about it? When was the last time you heard God and move on it?

# Seasons are Necessary

(a) When is the Season Necessary?

Seasons will not stop coming until we have completed our term on this earth. Nevertheless, this does not alter the fact that seasons are necessary in the lives of human beings and more so for the believer. Seasons are our teachers and they can cast a shadow of wisdom in our lives to share with someone else. This is one of the many reasons I believe seasons are necessary. For example, seasons take place when we have completed a period of time in our lives and even when a change is needed in your life. For the believer God controls the length of the season and He allows some things to take place in the season as a test of your faith. As I fore-stated there are teachable moments and critical lessons in each season. Seasons are necessary because they make room for progress and initiate new opportunities in our lives. A change in season not only means closure to the old season but, it creates opportunities for the new. Your thoughts are clearer and you can hear from the Lord as He ushers you into that necessary change. For that reason, allow the change to happen and consider it a much-needed makeover in life. In doing so, you will find the change to be a most definite rewarding experience. For this reason, there should be no more holding onto the old, just let it go. Again, let it go and welcome the change to a new and rewarding future.

*"And no one puts new wine into old wineskins. For the wine would burst the wineskins, and the wine and skins would both be lost. New wine calls for new wineskins" (Mark 2:22 NLT).*

Discuss the Seasons and how they bring about change

(b) Don't be afraid to Move in Your Season

Always remember to turn to God he will provide you with the means to move into your new season. Don't be afraid because God provided us with His only begotten son, Jesus Christ, so that we could have a new and abundant life. Peace is the opposite of fear because fear is the work of the devil. *"God has not given us the spirit of fear but of power and of love and of a sound mind" (2 Timothy 1:7 KJV).* Jesus said you don't have to worry about your life, what you will eat neither what you will drink, nor what you will wear. Your life is worth more to God than the birds in the air and they never worry about such things. Are you not much better than the birds of the air (Matthew 6:25-26)?

*"Can your worries add a single moment to your life? And why worry about your clothing? Look at the lilies of the field and how they grow; they don't work or make their clothing" (Matthew 6:27-28 NLT).*

Discuss: Fear and worry, what do you think will be the outcome of both?

# A New Beginning in Jesus

*Sandra E. Banks*

# A New Way of Teaching Life

Jesus taught the people a new way of doing things during his earthly ministry. He wanted to save people that did not think they needed to be saved. He showed them a different way of doing things that made a large number of them become upset and frustrated with him. They just didn't understand or even want to accept the new way Jesus was teaching because it meant that they had to change their way of thinking. Jesus gave knowledge, showed compassion, offered two-way communication, demonstrated forgiveness and became a servant to all because He is the savior of the world.

Jesus found it necessary and very important while on earth to fulfill His assignment as Messiah, as healer and as a high priest and teacher before he paid the ultimate price to redeem us on the cross at Calvary. With the disciples by his side and a multitude of people all around, Jesus began to teach and present several new ways to be effective followers of Christ. He started with a new way of giving (see Matthew 6:1-4) and Jesus taught his disciples a new way to pray (see Matthew 6:5-11). He implemented in His teaching how to forgive others (see Matthew 6:12-16). The Lord then taught us the proper way to serve (see Matthew 6:24). Last but not least, Jesus gave us a renewed mind to think clearly and have refreshing thoughts (see Matthew 6:31-34).

It is amazing that God so graciously sent His only begotten Son as our personal savior and teacher. Jesus taught lessons that will last until the end of this world as we know it. In accepting this task from His father, Jesus brought the world's purview into focus leaving each sinner with the question: what must I do to be saved?

Discuss: What is your understanding of Matthew 6:1-34?

*Sandra E. Banks*

# The Word of God Governs your Life

The word of God is a governing force in our lives and we must adhere to it as we travel on the straight and narrow pathway to life. God's word is dependable and it offers discipline and application to all life's situations. We depend on God's word because it is lasting and revives us when necessary. God's word is always clear and understandable and it has no flaws. We must put the word into practice, because that's where our strength lies. Most importantly the word of God remains pure from the past to the present and even into the future. God's word has cleansing and transforming power that persuades us to do His will. We must seek after this cleansing wholeheartedly.

*The scripture is a testament to the fact that "those whose hearts are completely His must obey Him" (2 Chronicles 16:9 KJV).*

Discuss: How would you express and characterize God's Word? Can you explain what it means to surrender completely to God?

*Sandra E. Banks*

# Conclusion

*Sandra E. Banks*

# Transforming Power

Jesus came to seek and to save the lost (the sinner man) therefore, we must accept His transforming power to do God's will. Transformation for believers is an on-going process and it is an action in progress. We have been clothed in Jesus' never-ending power. Our Plan of action in no uncertain terms is to spread the message of Jesus Christ to the lost. Scriptures have been identified that support the evil that lurks inside of man. Our thoughts become defiled by the evil such as; adultery, fornication, murder, theft, covetousness, wickedness, deceit, lasciviousness, envy, blasphemy, pride and foolishness, all come from within. God strongly supports the changing of the heart wholeheartedly. Once we have been transformed, by Jesus, we must remain focused on the will of God and what that really means. The big picture is to invest in God's son (Jesus Christ) who gave up His life for our freedom. We must begin to feed the plant (the seed) in the early morning; during the noon day and the evening because you don't know what place that investment (prayer in those times of day) will accomplish your desired outcome or produce the greater output. Jesus is your hope (seed-thought); He is where you make the investment. Jesus is your protector, deliverer, healer and comforter. He is responsible for feeding you, providing clothing and shelter too. He's never too busy to listen because He neither sleeps nor does He slumber. Take comfort in knowing that just as King Solomon thought it wise to invest in several commodities for the betterment of his kingdom, we too have someone even greater than King Solomon who invested in us.

Over 2000 years ago Jesus invested in our freedom, He said, *"Seek ye first the kingdom of God and His righteousness all these things shall be added unto you."* Jeremiah sent a letter to the people in exiles with these words, *"For I know the plans I have for you," says the LORD. I have plans to prosper you, not to harm you. I have plans to give you a future filled with hope."*

That hope today is Jesus Christ whom we can ask for anything. My last words to you were written by Paul the apostle, *"Do not conform to the pattern of this world, but be transformed by the renewing of your mind. Then you will be able to test and approve what God's will is—his good, pleasing and perfect will."*

As I bring these messages to a close, I want you to know that God by his own wisdom and power sent His son, Jesus Christ, to be our hope seed. He gave the awesome responsibility to an unworthy person by the name of Saul to bring His message to the Gentiles so that we too could be included in His kingdom as His children. Today both pastors and theologians have recognized Paul (formerly Saul) as becoming one of the greatest apostles of all time. Paul had a personal encounter with Christ, which led to a complete transformation. His ability to do the work of God was not his own but, was by the permissive will of God through the power of the Holy Spirit. God prepared Paul for this great missionary journey in an effort to reach the masses of the world. His principle duty and primary focus was to explain the mystery of God's will. That plan was a divine plan to be explained to the Gentiles, which was set in motion by God. You can read about God's predestination for the Gentiles in the book of Ephesians Chapter 1.

Paul describes the church, in detail first as a body, then a temple, a mystery, a new man, a bride and finally as a soldier. God gives the church awesome power in the hope of its calling by the power of the Holy Spirit. God predestinated us, He chose us, He accepted us, He adopted us, and God blesses us. Predestination means that God had a plan for us. God chose us before the foundation of the world. We are accepted by God through Jesus Christ because Jesus redeemed us, cleansed and forgave us and placed us back in fellowship with God. This is the hope we can depend on. *"For in hope we were saved, but hope that is seen is no hope at all. Who hopes for what he already has? But if we hope for what we do not yet have, we wait for it patiently" (Romans 8:24-25).*

Last but not least God blesses us with Spiritual blessings in heavenly places in Christ. Our hope is secure through our faith and with that faith we can see the invisible, believe the unbelievable and receive the impossible. We have that same power working in us as when God raised Jesus from the dead. As I close remember to use the power God gave you to exercise your faith and when you do, hope will become a manifestation of a reality in progress for you. Hope is a Seed Thought and Jesus is the Seed of hope. Pray always that you receive the blessings of God.

*"In the morning sow your seed and in the evening do not withhold your hand; For you do not know which will prosper, either this or that or whether both alike will be good" (Ecclesiastes 11:6 NKJV)*

*Sandra E. Banks*

# Closing Prayer

Dear heavenly Father I thank you for everyone who choose to read this book of inspiration. My hope is that as each individual reads, he or she will have true faith and believe that they will receive the promises of God. I pray each reader will see the blessings in store for them (from a distance) before they received them. And hopefully all will strive to be a faithful hearer and doer of God's holy word. All these things may seem as if the focus is on the earthly, but dear LORD God our true hope is for Jesus to return and receive us into His kingdom, as He himself promised

Finally my heavenly Father, please strengthen us with your power and might in making a conscious effort to give glory to you by honoring, praising and worshiping you, our God in sincerity on a daily basis. In Jesus name I ask it all, Amen.

# NOTES

*Sandra E. Banks*

# Supporting Scriptures

*Matthew 7:8*
*Ecclesiastes 11:6*
*Ephesians 6:18*
*Galatians 6:9*
*Romans 8:24-25*
*Jeremiah 17:7*
*Hebrews 6:11-12*
*Matthew 21:22*
*Philippians 4:6*
*Psalm 27:14*
*James 5:8*
*Philippians 4:8*
*Galatians 9:9*
*Proverbs 3:5-6*
*Psalm 126:5-6*
*Romans 2:11*
*Proverbs 28:21*
*Mark 11:24*
*I Thessalonians 5:11*
*James 5:16*
*Romans 12:12*
*I Corinthians 10:13*
*Proverbs 29:11*
*Proverbs 4:7*
*Psalm 54:4*
*James 1:19-20*
*Ecclesiastes 11:2*
*Ephesians 6:12*
*Mark 11:22*

*I Peter 5:7*
*Hebrews 11:6*
*Matthew 6:33*
*Matthew 6:25*
*John 15:7*
*Numbers 23:19*
*Philippians 4:12-13*
*Luke 4:28*
*John 8:12*
*John 8:32*
*Ephesians 5:8-9*
*Isaiah* 54:4-5
Romans 1:20
Matthew 8:8
Luke 4:13
Psalm 1:1
John 8:10-11
Genesis 12:1-2
II Corinthians 10:5
Mark 2:22
Matthew 6:27-28
Matthew 6:1-16
Matthew 6:24
Matthew 6:31-34
II Chronicles 16:9
Romans 12:2
II Chronicles 16:9

**Sandra Etienne Banks-Gordon** is available for author interviews. For more information contact us at info@advbooks.com

This book is available anywhere books are sold or visit our online store at **advbookstore.com.**

www.ingramcontent.com/pod-product-compliance
Lightning Source LLC
LaVergne TN
LVHW021525080426
835509LV00018B/2665